VANGUA...

David Harrison

S.B. Publications

First published in 2009 by S.B. Publications
14 Bishopstone Road, Seaford, East Sussex
Tel: 01323 893498   Email: sbpublications@tiscali.co.uk

© David Harrison 2009

No part of this publication may be reproduced, stored in a retrieval
system or transmitted by any means without the prior
permission of the copyright holder or publisher.

ISBN 978-185770-3467

Designed and Typeset by EH Graphics, East Sussex (01273) 515527

CONTENTS

Vanguard Way 4

Introduction 5

SECTION ONE
Croydon to Limpsfield Chart (14 miles/22.5km) 9

SECTION TWO
Limpsfield Chart to Forest Row (12½ miles/20km) 15

SECTION THREE
Forest Row to Blackboys (13¾ miles/22km) 21

SECTION FOUR
Blackboys to Alfriston (14 miles/22.5km) 27

SECTION FIVE
Alfriston to Newhaven (9¾ miles/15.6km) 35

VANGUARD WAY

This 66-mile (105km) walk links East Croydon in Surrey with Newhaven on the south coast. It was devised in 1980 by members of the Vanguards Rambling Club which was based in Croydon and begins at East Croydon railway station. After leaving the town it passes through Littleheath Wood before reaching Selsdon, beyond which it negotiates Selsdon Wood on its way to Farleigh Court and Chelsham. Now it crosses the North Downs and skirts Titsey Park before crossing the Greensand Ridge at Limpsfield Chart. A short incursion into Kent follows the Eden valley before returning to Surrey and passing the moat which is all that remains of Starborough Castle. Not far now to the Sussex Border Path, proceeding ever southwards through the High Weald into Forest Row and Ashdown Forest. Beyond Gill's Lap and King's Standing it penetrates ever deeper into East Sussex, through High Hurstwood and past Pound Green to Blackboys and the start of the Low Weald.

Passing Arlington Reservoir it visits the remarkably colourful church at Berwick before dropping through the Cuckmere valley to Alfriston, whose great church is called the Cathedral of the Downs. The route along the Cuckmere is shared with the South Downs Way, through Litlington and across the Downs past Charleston Manor before dropping down into the lovely little village of Westdean. Reaching the main coast road at the Seven Sisters Country Park the route proceeds to Exceat Bridge then on towards the fishermen's cottages at the foot of Seaford Head. The final section heads west along the cliff top down into Seaford, continuing along the promenade past the Martello Tower and beyond Tide Mills to the Harbour at Newhaven.

The variation of scenery en route is truly remarkable and the closing section from Alfriston is nothing short of sensational!

INTRODUCTION

This guide splits the walk into five sections for no particular reason other than the fact that they divide it up into five similar distances mileage wise. Not that each section is intended to represent a day's walking, for everyone walks at a different pace; not that each section is devised because it ends with a convenient transport link, because they don't; nor do they necessarily provide overnight accommodation, for the route passes through some pretty remote country, dotted in some cases with only the odd farm or cottage. Where public transport exists it is mentioned in the text, but it is always advisable to confirm its availability before travelling. Overnight accommodation ideally should be pre-booked and Tourist Information Offices can help with this. The Croydon office (Tel: 020 8253 1009) in Katherine Street were particularly helpful, but alas at the time of writing were under the threat of closure. Simon Kerr, Tourism and Information Officer at East Grinstead Town Council located at the Library Building in West Street (Tel: 01342 410121) is not only helpful but extremely enthusiastic about what he does and will help all he can. The only other Tourist Information Office on the route is at Seaford (Tel: 01323 897426) near the end of the walk.

The ideal option is to decide on the length of a day's walk and have two cars, one parked waiting at the end of the proposed walk so that your party can drive back to retrieve the other car left parked at the beginning of the day's walk. Or, if like me, you have an understanding partner, they can drop you off at the start of the day's walk and pick you up at the pre-arranged point later in the day.

Alternatively you can back-pack, carrying all your belongings with you, although finding somewhere to pitch a tent may not be to everyone's liking.

However you decide to cover the route you will find it is not particularly well signposted, other than at the beginning and the end. By following this guide the indecision of where to go and which way to decide when the route divides is not a problem. If following a main path or track and others lead off in any direction always stick to the main route. If it is necessary to change direction the guide will direct you. If there is a special feature or structure useful as a landmark or identity characteristic it will draw your attention to it. Sometimes it gives distances (ie 100 yards/95m) or perhaps a few paces depending on the distance referred to. If there is a question of doubt it will always set you off in the right direction.

Much of the route is across farmland and along bridleways. It is as well to bear in mind that these sections can be extremely muddy in wet weather, making the going underfoot unpleasant and slippery and progress considerably slower than imagined and this should be taken into consideration when planning your outing.

Finally, a word about safety. The last section - and the most spectacular - is along the cliff top path from Cuckmere Haven to Seaford. It is important that you stick to the footpath along this stretch and keep well away from the cliff edge. The cliffs are chalk and break away very easily. Some detours are in place avoiding the more vulnerable cliff falls but they can occur at any time and it's a long way down!

And so to begin. By starting out from East Croydon railway station it makes sense to let the train take the strain, wherever you may be setting out from. Getting out of Croydon is much easier than you might imagine and far more pleasant - there are plenty of leafy alleys and woodland walks to begin with, and once over the M25 the peace and solitude set the scene for the remainder of the walk.

I hope you enjoy the experience. I'm sure you will.

Vanguard Way signpost, Seaford Bay.

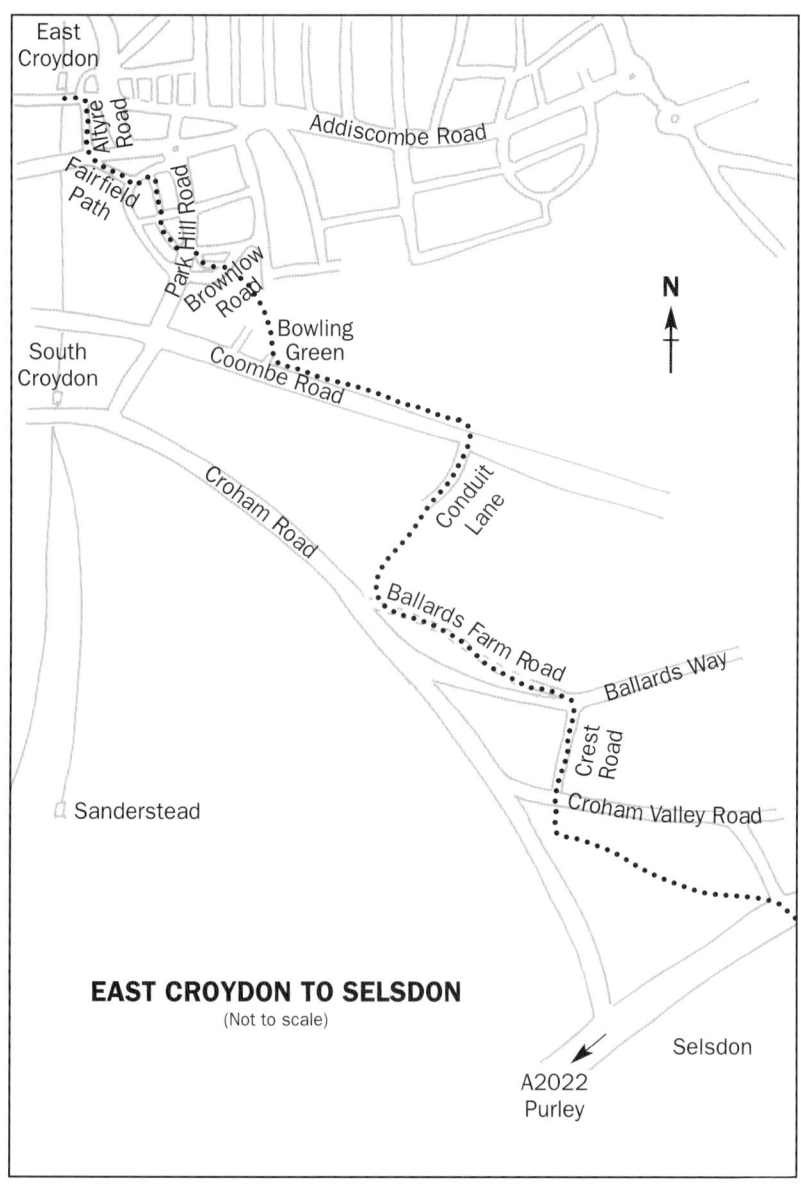

SECTION ONE

CROYDON TO LIMPSFIELD CHART
(14 miles/22.5km)

Being Surrey's largest town before being absorbed into Greater London, Croydon is no place to linger on an excursion such as this. But some old buildings do survive amid this fast-expanding commercial centre, including the brick-built almshouses dated 1599 which are little changed, nestling among the tall office blocks. Parts of the medieval Palace of the Archbishops of Canterbury still survive too, contrasting with the Fairfield Halls containing the Ashcroft Theatre and the Arnhem Gallery. But it is East Croydon railway station which sees the start of our journey, so it is this landmark we seek first. Then we have to negotiate leaving the built-up area of Croydon before making our way over the North Downs and the M25 to the Greensand Ridge at Limpsfield Chart.

Turn left out of the station, crossing the road and the tramway before turning right into Altyre Road. Cross over the dual carriageway and along Fairfield Path, with Parkhill School on the right, then turn right at the T-junction and left almost immediately into St Bernards, continuing along a pathway to Park Hill Road, which cross straight over. Turn off left in about 15 yards (14m) then uphill to the road, where bear right. Turn right by No. 1 and drop downhill, crossing Brownlow Road to continue along a pleasant alleyway between houses to Lloyd Park. Turn left round the bowling green then right, keeping a fenced off area to the right. Head diagonally right to the pavilion, crossing the tram tracks into Coombe Road, where turn left along an attractive walkway twixt tramway and road and passing the Premier Travel Inn on the right.

Turn right into Conduit Lane, where Coombe Gardens are on the corner, providing toilets and Tea Rooms. Keep ahead by Central Nursery where the metalled road becomes a track, continuing along an idyllic stretch of the route through Coombe Wood. Turn left at a signpost

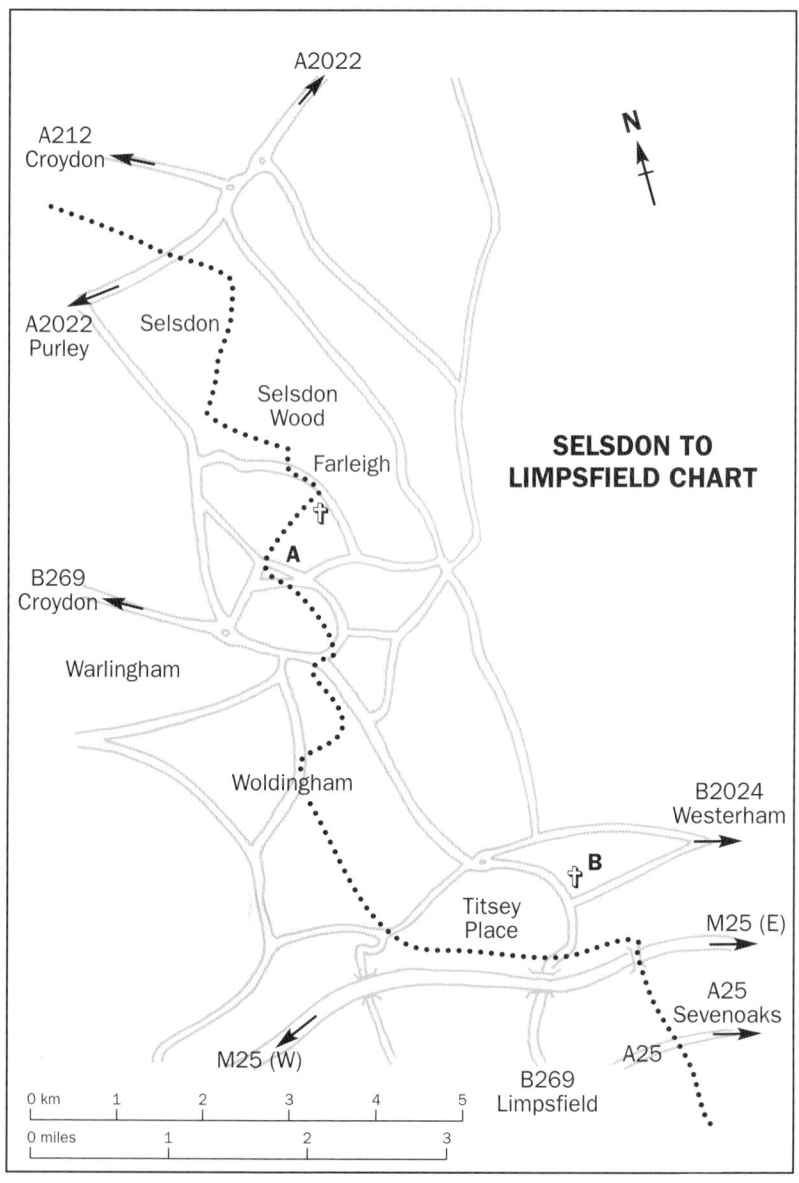

along a bridleway to Addington, (Ballards Farm Road), and at the road turn right and in 50 yards (48m) turn left into Crest Road. Cross straight over Croham Valley Road and along another alley, turning left midway along at the Vanguard Way signpost into Littleheath Wood. Keep ahead where the track divides, following the blue waymarkers right then left, ascending gently then descending and ascending again before passing a huge concrete water tower on the left. Where the path divides by the houses, take the right option and a blue waymarker soon confirms the route. Now cut down to the pylon and cross the A2022, continuing along Ashen Vale and keeping ahead at the public footpath signpost as the road swings off right, through the housing estate of Selsdon and into Selsdon Wood.

Bear right through the kissing gate into Selsdon Wood, following the signs for the London Loop and keeping to the main track through the wood to the clearing. Turn right at the clearing and back into the woods, crossing the entrance to Farleigh Court Golf Club before turning left along a track along the edge of a copse to the golf course. Turn right at the Vanguard Way waymarker, over a stile and along the track to

Church of St. Mary the Virgin at Farleigh, dating back to 1083.

the road at Farleigh Court. Turn left at the road and right into Church Road, passing the church of St Mary the Virgin at Farleigh, which dates back to 1083.

Leave the churchyard by the public bridleway over to the left, crossing straight over at the cross-tracks, under the bridge and turn right opposite the school into Chelsham (**A**). The village church stands alone about a mile (1.6km) to the east and is mainly thirteenth century with traces of Norman work. Three yew trees stand in its churchyard, each over nine feet (3m) round, planted by the rector and schoolmaster in 1746.

Turn off left beside the bus stop, continuing straight across the road in the direction of the Vanguard Way waymarker, past the Bull Inn and keeping ahead across the green to the road. Turn left at the road and right at the public bridleway immediately before the crossroads with the wood on the right. Keep ahead to the road where turn right, and as it meets the B269 on the outskirts of Warlingham, turn right again, then left in 80 yards (76m) at the public footpath signpost, through the wood to the left of the cottage. Over the stile and ahead across the next field, keeping to the left of the quarry and past the dew pond before heading diagonally left towards the rear of the big house, where turn sharp right down the hill, crossing the track to the road. Turn left at the road, taking the footpath off left as the road swings off right, through the wood and heading towards the telecommunication masts on top of the North Downs along a good track. Keep ahead to the road by Flint House, where stay ahead signposted Oxted, turning off left at the footpath signpost as the road starts to dip. Follow the path round to the left, crossing a stile and heading diagonally left down Oxted Down to join the North Downs Way and the Pilgrims Way, which at this point are one and the same. Pass through a metal kissing gate as the route now runs parallel with the M25 on the right, past a plaque indicating the point where the North Downs Way and the Vanguard Way pass from the western to the eastern hemisphere.

Go down some steps into a gully where the North Downs Way and the Vanguard Way go their separate ways; North Downs Way to the left and the Vanguard Way to the right. Follow the track down and across the access road to Titsey Place by Pitchfont Lodge, continuing ahead a few steps beyond the lodge to a stile off left which cross before heading diagonally right across the field to another stile by a metal gate. Cross the next field to another stile by a lone tree, then across two more fields to the road, where half-mile (800m) to the left stands Titsey church (**B**). This section will be very muddy in wet weather!

The Romans built a villa in Titsey Park and the church has a family chapel connected with those who lived at the great house and there are several memorials to the Greshams and the Leverson-Gowers who came after them. The oldest is the brass portrait of William Gresham kneeling at prayer with his wife and seven children. He was a first cousin of Thomas Gresham who founded the Royal Exchange and, like him, died in 1579. His grandson John is remembered by a big memorial, which greets you as you enter. Sir Marmaduke, of 1742, also had a son named John who is remembered for a different reason. He pulled down the house of his ancestors and also the fourteenth century church, because it stood too near to the new house he was building. Today's church is the eighteenth century successor, with tiles the only survivor from the old church. Turn left at the B269 and in 100 yards (95m) turn off right, just round the bend in the road. Keep ahead across the field to a public footpath signpost by the M25 where turn left, keeping parallel with the motorway before climbing the steps to join a bridleway. Turn right here over the motorway before skirting Titsey Wood on the left and then a sandpit on the right.

Cross straight over the A25, descending Watts Hill and passing through a little metal gate and then a wooden gate before keeping ahead at the cross-tracks on entering the wood. Bear up right, keeping open land to the right. A marker post soon confirms the route, forking right and following blue waymarkers to the road, which cross straight over, along a shingle path and then a road to the church at Limpsfield Chart (**C**). Close by is a house fashioned from the old Salt Box days of medieval times, where salt was stored before its distribution, and on the lovely common Baden-Powell and Colonel Cody used to fly man-lifting kites in the days when man first had the inkling to fly.

The Carpenters Arms public house is off to the right by the green.

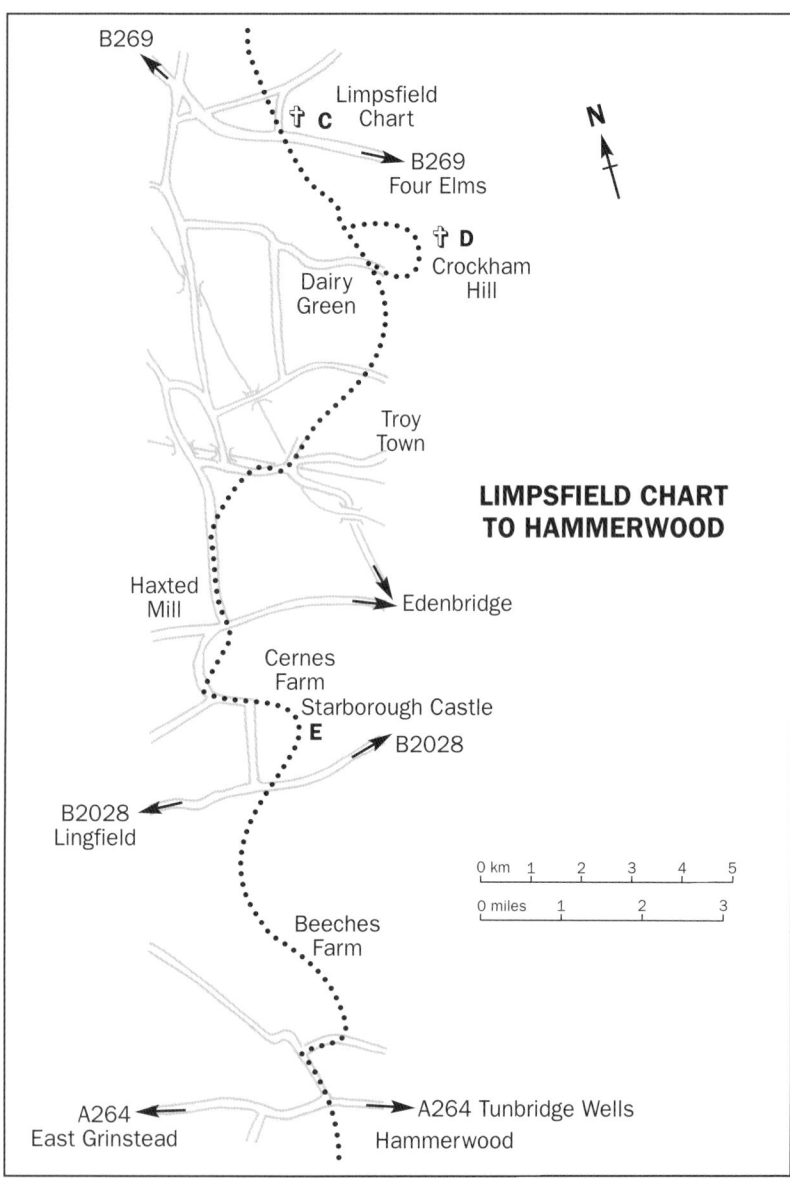

SECTION TWO

LIMPSFIELD CHART TO FOREST ROW
(12¹/₂ miles/20km)

This second section takes the Way into three counties; passing from Surrey into Kent briefly before returning to Surrey and the Eden valley, then crosses into East Sussex on its way through the High Weald to Forest Row.

From the church at Limpsfield Chart proceed down Trevereux Hill opposite, forking right where the path splits and continue on down the hill. The track bends right by a house with a lake and just before it bends back left, turn off left over a stile to a cross-tracks by a tree. Here there is a choice of route. Turn right to a stile just to the left of the oast house, then follow a well-used path over two more stiles to the road, where turn left past Hurst Farm to Dairy Green. Or, alternatively, to take a mile (1.6km) detour to visit the lovely Kent village of Crockham Hill (**D**) with its magnificent views from one of the highest points in the county.

Here in the church is the tomb of Octavia Hill, one of the founders of the National Trust, and here also is a window in memory of Richard Warde of nearby Squerryes Court who built the church. But it is the view that everyone comes here to see. To make the detour, keep straight ahead at the tree, past the lake and through the small copse to reach the road in the village. Turn right to the crossroads then left at the pub to visit the church. The way back to the main route goes off right at the crossroads, along a lane which leads back to the road where a right turn joins back up with the Vanguard Way at Dairy Green.

At the entrance to Dairy Green cross over the stile immediately on the left, and at the start of the wood cross another stile to the right, keeping the wood on the left. Cross yet another stile, now with the wood on the right, following the path round left still with Guildables Wood on the right. Turn off right at the end of the wood, still keeping alongside it on the right and then ahead over open field to the road. Turn left at the road and in a few paces right. Go through the metal gates and along an enclosed path off right and at the lane turn left into Troy Town. At the T-junction turn right over the railway, then right down Honeypot Lane. Cross the bridge over Kent Brook, ignoring the footpath off left alongside it, but almost immediately turn off left at the stile beside the entrance to Ash Farm back into Surrey. Over a series of stiles negotiating the paddocks before turning left through a metal gate and across a field to the road. Turn left at the road to the T-junction where turn right, past Haxted Mill, an eighteenth century weatherboarded water mill and restaurant on the River Eden. Turn left over the stile by the river, crossing the bridge as the river makes a sharp turn and then head diagonally left to the road.

Turn left over the bridge, keeping ahead and ignoring the road off right and staying ahead as the road then turns sharp right. Leave the second field by a stile in the top right corner by Cernes Farm, turning right down the lane and in 25 yards (24m) turn off left over a stile. Half-way along the edge of the field turn off left over a stile by the public footpath

The 18th century Haxted Mill on the River Eden.

signpost, turning right to continue along the drive of Starborough Castle (**E**).

The castle was founded by Reginald de Cobham in 1341 and was rectangular with four round towers surmounted by strange domes. After distinguishing himself at Poitiers, de Cobham became a knight of the garter and was made Lord High Admiral. His son Reginald fought at Agincourt and was entrusted with the captured Duke of Orleans - who later became Louis XII - at Starborough. Louis spent twenty years here before being ransomed. After the Reigate affair of 1648 the castle was demolished by Parliament and the moat is all that remains of it today.

Continue ahead along the track, soon turning off right across the corner of the field at the public footpath to the B2028, where turn right. In 20 yards (19m) turn off left, opposite the road off right to Haxted. At the cross-tracks turn right and then left in 20 yards (19m) to resume the original direction. Turn right at the wide track and left by the cottages, skirting on the left the ancient site of Dry Hill fort. Turn left at Beeches Farm then right down a concrete track soon to become a metalled lane. Turn right at the road, and left at the T-junction to the A264. Cross straight over here to continue along another track, turning off left as the track swings off right, meeting a bridleway at the end of the wood. Turn right here and through the tail end of Hammerwood before passing under the power lines. At the track turn right at Dog Gate Lodge past Owlett's Farm, following the track round left past Hirstbrook House, shown on the map as Thornhill. Keep left where the track splits by Holmfield Cottage, turning off right at the entrance to Surries Farm and staying ahead as the road comes in from the right. Turn off right along the public footpath as the road bends round left. Under more power lines and along the edge of a wood , keeping ahead through the car park and on to the B2110 in Forest Row (**F**).

The gateway to Ashdown Forest; for it was here the hunting lodges were built to house the royal hunting parties after a hard day in the saddle and it was not until the railway was opened in 1866 that there was any substantial development in the area, achieving full parish status in 1894. The railway is no more and the track has been turned into a country trail. On its eastward section towards East Grinstead it passes the ruins of Brambletye House, built in 1631 for Sir Henry Compton. Half a century later it was owned by Sir James Richards who, while out hunting one day in the Forest, was warned that he was suspected of treason and that his house was to be searched. He took immediate flight to the coast, taking a boat to Spain and returning to Brambletye no more. It is said that since that day when Sir James passed through the gatehouse the house has never been tenanted since. Horace Smith renewed interest in the place with his famous historical romance in 1826, a book much admired by Sir Walter Scott, and the name lives on in the Brambletye Hotel which was featured in Sir Arthur Conan Doyle's *Black Peter* when Sherlock Holmes spent some time here. The hotel has a 'Black Peter's Bar' to this day.

Another interesting building is Kidbrooke Park, built in 1724 for Lord Abergavenny after his Eridge Park estate was destroyed by fire. It has seen many owners, including Charles Abbot, Speaker of the House of Commons at the beginning of the nineteenth century and Olaf Hambro, chairman of Hambros Bank who bought the house in 1921. He helped finance an expedition to the Himalayas by Kingdon-Ward who brought back a blue poppy which the late Queen Mary, wife of George V, came to Forest Row to see. Hambro sold the house in 1938 after the death of his wife and it became a school. It is not open to public view.

Another educational establishment given the royal seal of approval was Ashdown House preparatory school, when it was chosen by Princess Margaret and Lord Snowdon for their son Viscount Linley, and the couple were regular visitors to the village while he was a pupil there.

Toilets and refreshment facilities available at several venues in the village, for which turn right at the B2110.

Public Transport: Route 729 to Tunbridge Wells operates hourly (Monday to Saturday) and 2 hourly on Sundays with connecting service Route 291 to Forest Row every 2 hours (except Sunday). Check times of buses before travelling.

General view of Ashdown Forest from Broadstone car park.

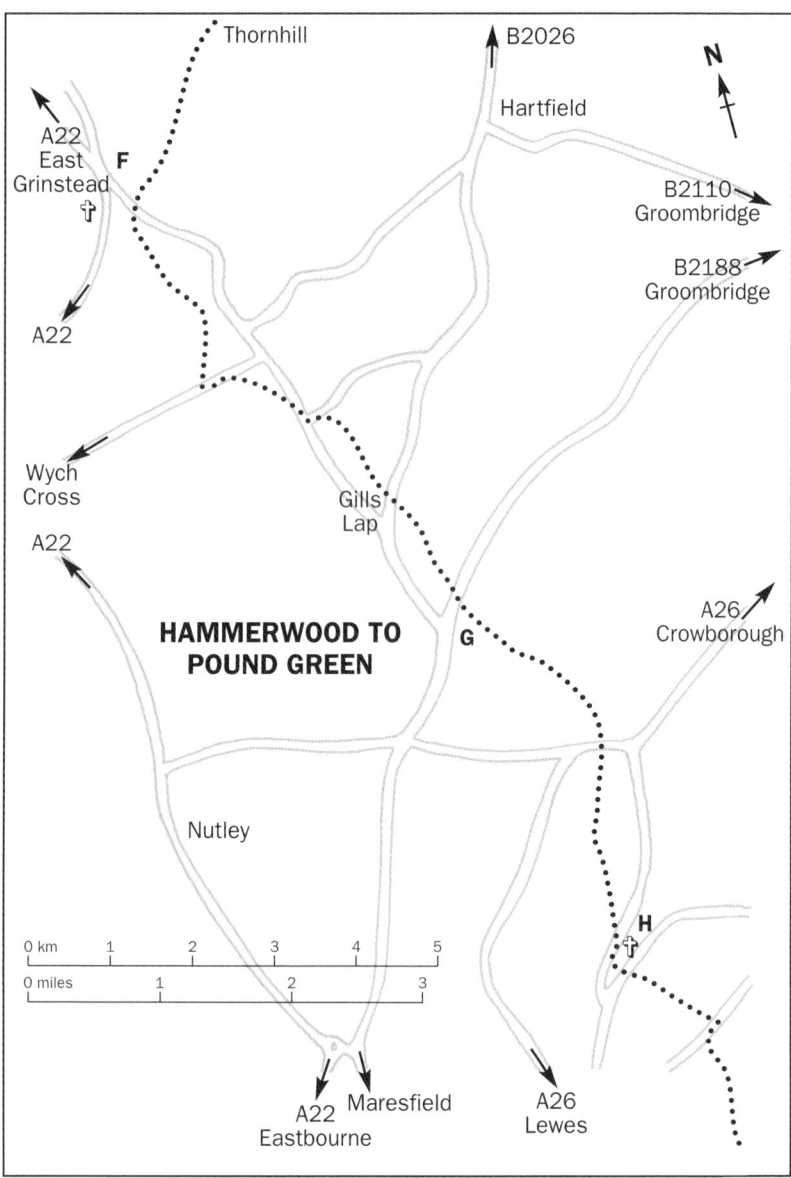

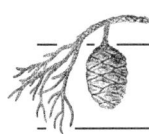

SECTION THREE

FOREST ROW TO BLACKBOYS
(13³/₄ miles/22km)

In this section the route remains in East Sussex, starting off in the High Weald, crossing Ashdown Forest and finishing in the Wealden village of Blackboys. The landscape is clear and open, for Ashdown Forest is forest in name only, its trees long since felled to fuel the furnaces of the Sussex iron industry that was rife in this part of England in the sixteenth century. But this ponders the question why were the trees not regenerated if their supply was so important. With the iron industry here in decline come the beginning of the nineteenth century, it is much more likely that all the grazing animals belonging to the commoners polished off the trees with nobody bothering to replant in their wake. Apathy, it would seem, is not a modern complaint after all!

From Forest Row proceed east along the B2110, past the Foresters Arms before following a tarmac path from School Lane across Ashdown Road and up right along an alley then right into Chapel Lane. Turn off left at the Vanguard Way signpost opposite Garden House, turning left at the Royal Ashdown Forest Golf Club. Cross the stream and into the wood, turning right at the driveway and continuing left along the edge of the golf course, with trees on the left. At the fence follow the boundary of the golf course a further 100 yards (95m) before turning off left into the trees, continuing straight across the metalled track and along a public bridleway to the road. Turn left here and in 200 yards (190m) turn right at a bridleway, crossing a metalled lane to a cricket pitch which follow round left, forking off right at the end of it. Follow a good track round left to meet another road, where turn right. Cross the river and turn left at the next road junction, over the ford and turning off it to the right almost immediately along a fire ride. The route from here is indecisive, but by turning left at the first T-junction, right at the second T-junction, left at the cross-tracks and right at the bench the Way emerges at Gills Lap car park.

A stretch of Vanguard Way in Ashdown Forest

Cross the B2026 by the T-junction, bearing right and proceeding parallel with the main road beyond where the Wealdway crosses to Pines car park. Continue on, crossing the B2188 and keeping ahead behind King's Standing (**G**).

It was here that a raised hide was situated, presumably in the clump still visible, which became a feature of the type of hunting that became popular in late Tudor times. The *Standing,* or raised shooting box, was a tall open-sided structure from which the royal and noble huntsmen would be ensconced. For instead of the old familiar method of chasing deer on horseback the hunters would shoot with bow and arrow or gun at the deer as they were driven past the *Standing* by keepers.

Keep to the bridleway as it makes its way off left, following it all the way to the A26 at Oldbell House, where turn left. Cross the road just before the Crow and Gate public house and over the stile behind the bus stop. Over two more stiles to a field behind the cottages where turn right to another stile in the top right corner. Bear right to yet another stile, then turn left along an enclosed path into Newnham Park Wood.

Turn right at the public footpath signpost and left onto a concrete track, turning off in a few paces through a small gate by another public footpath signpost. Look out for another signpost where turn off left, up ten steps and along the edge of Stroods boundary. Through a metal gate and along the right edge of the next field, crossing a stile on the right at the gap through into the next field. LOOK OUT FOR THIS STILE - IT IS EASY TO MISS! Follow the path down right, crossing a series of wooden walkways before hitting the road where turn right, downhill, before turning left to the church at High Hurstwood (**H**).

Early seventeenth century recordings of this village suggest that the origins of the name isn't 'high' but 'hay' meaning hedge - hence the hedged hurst or wood. The church of Holy Trinity, next to the dell with rhododendrons of the parsonage garden, was built 1870-2 with a bellcote on the west end of the chancel and has a lower apse. The south tower with its half-timbered top storey was added in 1903.

Turn right just before the church, through a kissing gate, turning left at the road and in 100 yards (95m) turn right at the public bridleway

Church of Holy Trinity at High Hurstwood, built 1870-2.

signpost. Follow the track, bearing off left at Hurstwood Farm, then forking right. Keep ahead at Holders Farm, crossing the stile just left of the farm entrance and along an enclosed path, crossing the stream and turning right alongside it. Cross another stream before heading diagonally left across the next field to a stile beside a metal gate. Turn right at the road, past the entrance to Greenhurst Farm, and in 100 yards (95m) turn off left over a stile, following the path under the railway bridge. Keep ahead at the cross-tracks and on to the A272. Cross straight over and turn immediately left onto a track beside Pound Cottage, continuing ahead along the path to a road where turn right, taking the right fork where the road divides as far as the crossroads. Turn left here and in 50 yards (48m) turn right, over the stile at the public footpath, bearing left through a wood and keeping ahead at the cross-tracks. Over a stream and through a small metal gate before turning to the left of a copse, following the path through a messy scrapyard and turning left at the public footpath signpost by the building. Keep right where the path divides, keeping to the main track to the road, where turn right, turning left at the next track at the public bridleway sign in 100 yards (95m). Keep ahead, passing the lake on the left where the Wealdway comes in from the right, into the start of Tickerage Wood. Soon look for the turning off left, turning left again at the T-junction and right in 20 yards (19m) at the public footpath signpost. Turn off left through the allotments to the village hall, turning right at the road and keeping straight across at the crossroads into Blackboys (**I**).

There are several derivatives as to why this village is so named. Local legend has it that it is accredited to the 'black boys' or charcoal burners from the local iron foundries who used the fourteenth century Blackboys Inn to slake their thirst at the end of the day. It has also been suggested that the name means either 'Black Wood' or 'Blake's Wood', but there is nothing to substantiate this on the map. There is record of a Richard Blakeboy living in the village in 1398 and proof that the village was actually called Blakeboyes in 1437.

Whatever the true reason is behind its fascinating name there is no disguising the fact that its inn was clearly a posting stage for coaches travelling from London through Uckfield and on to Hastings, and on the opposite side of the now residential road beside the inn is a group of cottages which look very much like converted stables. It had an illustrious landlord too, for Ronald Shiner, the actor who starred in a string of films and West End farces including *Worm's Eye View* in the 1950s, retired from the stage to become mine host here.

Blackboys Inn dating back to the 14th century.

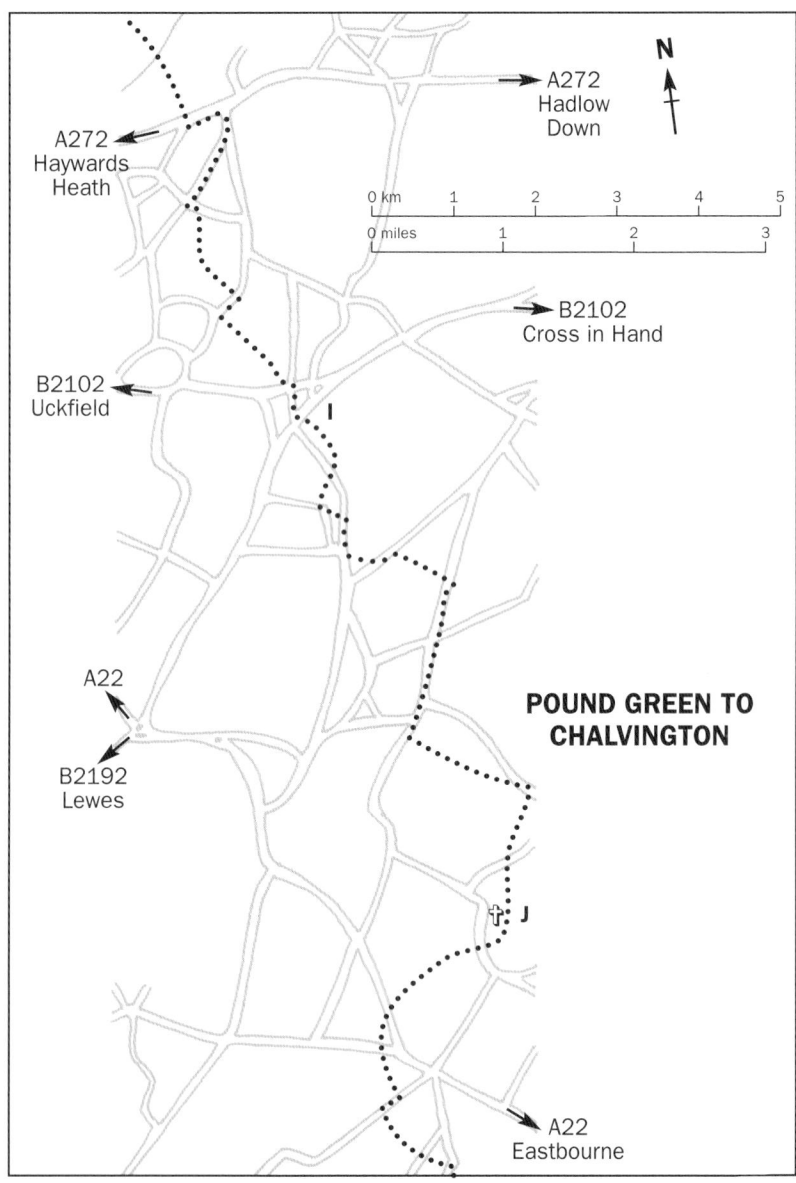

SECTION FOUR

BLACKBOYS TO ALFRISTON
(14 miles/22.5km)

Now the route passes into the Low Weald, converging once again with the Wealdway at Chiddingly and passing close by Arlington Reservoir by Berwick Station. Just across the A27 is Berwick village, whose church is amazingly colourful thanks to the labours of some well-known parishioners from nearby Charleston Farmhouse. From here it is but a stone's throw to Alfriston, a delightfully pretty little village, whose church is known as the Cathedral of the Downs.

From the inn cross the B2192, turn right and in a few paces turn left alongside Kiln Wood, following the yellow waymarkers round right. Down the steps and across the stream before turning right to the road, where turn left. Turn off right as the road swings off left beside Bushmere. At the next road turn left, and as the road swings off right by Pear Tree Cottage, keep ahead onto the public footpath. At the road turn right and opposite Beechy Road turn off left, heading diagonally right across the field to the tip of the wood where turn right alongside it to the road. At the road turn left and in 100 yards (95m) turn right, turning left at the open field and through the gap into the next field, where turn right and on to the road by Moat Farm.

Turn right here, following the road straight ahead at the crossroads, under the power lines to the junction off right opposite Gray Wood House. Turn left opposite this junction into the wood, crossing the track and keeping ahead along a well-used path, passing a summer camping site on the left. At the track turn left to the road and here turn right, turning right again where the public footpath crosses the road. Turn right where the path meets the road, then left in a few paces, meeting the road again, and the Wealdway, and the Chiddingly pub by Chiddingly church (**J**).

The -ly ending to the village name denotes that it is of Saxon origin and means it was originally a cleared area of woodland, here belonging

The church at Chiddingly has one of only three stone spires in Sussex and at 130ft (40m) is considered to be the best.

to a Saxon tribal group called the Cittingas and their leader would have been Citta. It is recorded in Domesday Book as *Cetelingei* and became known as Chittinly in the seventeenth century.

In a humble way the village is said to resemble Rome, for its parish rests upon seven hills, but there was nothing humble about the Jefferay family, the old lords of the manor. They were so proud it was said their feet never touched the ground on the way from their mansion, Chiddingly Place, to the church, stepping on cheeses used as stepping stones to save their feet from getting soiled. Within the church is a series of tombs to the Jefferay family, culminating in a monument 18 feet (5.5m) high showing Sir John Jefferay lying on a pillow in his ermine robes, his wife below him, their daughter and her husband at the side and their son in front. Unfortunately it has been badly defaced, the reason being, so the story goes, that somebody mistook Sir John for Judge Jeffreys of 'Bloody Assize' infamy.

The church also stands proud for having one of only three stone spires in Sussex. Standing 130 feet (40m) high and recently restored it is also considered to be the best. From the back of the churchyard take the footpath round the cricket pitch to the road which cross, bearing diagonally left across the field to a gate, then over a stile and into the wood. Turn left at the cross-tracks signpost, then diagonally right across the next field. Look for the signpost in the middle of the next field, keeping straight ahead then maintaining a more or less straight line through a couple of metal gates to the A22.

At the A22 turn left and in 100 yards (95m) opposite Holmes Hill House turn off right along a short stretch of footpath to the B2124. Cross straight over here, continuing along a track which soon divides. Take the left option here, passing to the left of the house, then right alongside a stream to the road. Cross straight over, skirting Deanland Wood on the right, then following another stream to a road. Turn right here then left in 100 yards (95m) to Limekiln Farm, continuing ahead as the track swings right, just past the seat to a lane where turn right. Follow this long straight lane past Mount Pleasant Farm, keeping ahead along the byway as the lane peters out to the road on the outskirts of Chalvington (**K**).

Although the route doesn't actually visit the village, it will be of interest to all cricket fans to know that the cricket pitch here, behind the Yew Tree Inn, is reputed to be the oldest in the country. In the nineteenth century Sussex used it for their county games and even England played here once, albeit the national ladies' team under Rachel Heyhoe-Flint, when they took on Ripe and Chalvington CC.

Continue along the next stretch of road, passing under a double set of power lines and veering right at the T-junction. Just past North Mays House on the left turn off left, crossing the next two fields diagonally right to the corrugated farm building at Mays Farm. Continue to the left of the farm as far as the little metal gate in front of the impressive looking farmhouse. Through the gate and head diagonally right across the field, heading for the stile in the top right corner of the next field. Bear left past Ludlay House and along a lane, turning off right over a stile where Arlington Reservoir (**L**) now comes into view.

It was completed by Eastbourne Water Company in 1971 and

The impressive farmhouse at Mays Farm.

supplies over five million gallons of water daily. Private trout fishing is permissible and the reservoir when full holds 770 million gallons to a depth of 37 feet (11m). It was formed by cutting off a meander in the river and damming one end. The remains of prehistoric animals were found during its excavation and over 30,000 trees were planted on its completion, including oak, birch, wild cherry, mountain ash and hawthorn.

At the road turn right, crossing the railway at Berwick station (**M**) by the Berwick Inn and turning off right onto a bridleway beside the green corrugated building and heading diagonally left across the next field.

The story behind this station is quite a tale! In the early days of the twentieth century Horatio Bottomley, MP was squire of The Dicker, a village a couple of miles (3.2km) up the road, and many remember him with affection. But for all that he was a rogue and a scoundrel who loved women and making money. An orphan, he made a fortune through newspapers and publishing, for he was a financial wizard, brilliant orator and prize swindler. He rigged competitions, fixed lotteries and in 1922 appeared at the Old Bailey on 24 different fraudulent charges for which he was found guilty and sent to prison for seven years. That was his undoing, for he came out of prison a broken man and died four years later penniless.

But during his heyday he built much of the village and bought up much of what was already there, for the great wealth he amassed was not used only for his own purpose. He was a very generous man - he could afford to be - and built himself a mansion which had the only telephone in the village and then allowed everyone else to use it. He threw lavish parties.... But what has all this to do with a railway station, you ask? He was so influential that he persuaded the railway company to build Berwick Station so that all his cronies could get easy access from London to attend his parties. That is the original reason for a station at this point, and the mansion that Bottomley was so proud of is now St Bede's public school, The Dicker.

Trains to Lewes, London and Eastbourne. Check train information on 08457 48 49 50 www.nationalrail.co.uk

At Stonery Farm turn off left onto another bridleway to the road, which cross straight over, heading diagonally left over the next fields before turning right along the right edge of the field to the A27. Turn left here then right at the crossroads into Berwick village (**N**).

Turn off left by The Cricketers, whose pub sign caused quite a stir when it was in need of replacing. Imagine the reaction on entering the church when, during the Second World War, the Bishop of Chichester commissioned local artists Duncan Grant, Vanessa Bell and her son Quentin Bell to paint contemporary murals on the walls of the twelfth century parish church. Their startling pictures include a soldier, sailor and airman, the Annunciation and the Nativity and incorporate the portraits of local personalities. Note the Sussex features, including the well-laden trug basket in the Nativity. Trug baskets are made at nearby Herstmonceux and have been a traditional craft in Sussex for almost two hundred years. The angels above the chancel arch all have impeccable Forties style hair-do's.

On a more serious note the church can bear testimony to the fact that lightning can strike twice in the same place, for in 1774 the spire was struck and destroyed and in 1982 considerable damage was caused to the repaired structure when it was struck again.

Leave the churchyard and turn right, crossing the bridle path to continue along the public footpath, which eventually joins the bridle path again before meeting the metalled road, which follow ahead into Alfriston (**O**). There are public toilets in the car park, which is passed on the left just before the market cross.

Once a Saxon settlement this lovely downland village is justifiably known as the Capital of the Downs. Its fine square boasts the traditional spreading chestnut tree and a battered market cross, unique in East Sussex and rivalled only by a better example in Chichester in the entire county. It was probably erected in the 15th century for Henry IV granted Tuesday market rights in 1405. The cross was hit by a lorry in 1955 and so badly damaged only a small portion of the original stone could be used in its replacement.

Buildings either side of the High Street display all the main characteristic materials of the area; timber frames filled with daub and plaster or covered by weather-boarding or rich, red tiles. Here 14th and 15th century houses, tearooms, shops and restaurants jostle for position along with four inns of unique character, the most renowned being the Star Inn which has been everything in its time from a resting place for pilgrims to a haunt for smugglers.

The Old Clergy House was the first property bought by the National Trust for £10 in 1896. It stands on the edge of the Tye (an old Saxon name for village green) which is dominated by the church of St Andrews, known because of its size as the Cathedral of the Downs. Built about 1360 it is unlike any of its counterparts being constructed all at one time with no later additions. Its list of rectors and vicars go back to 1272 which would suggest an earlier Saxon church occupied the same site although there is no mention in Domesday Book to verify this.

Alfriston Church.

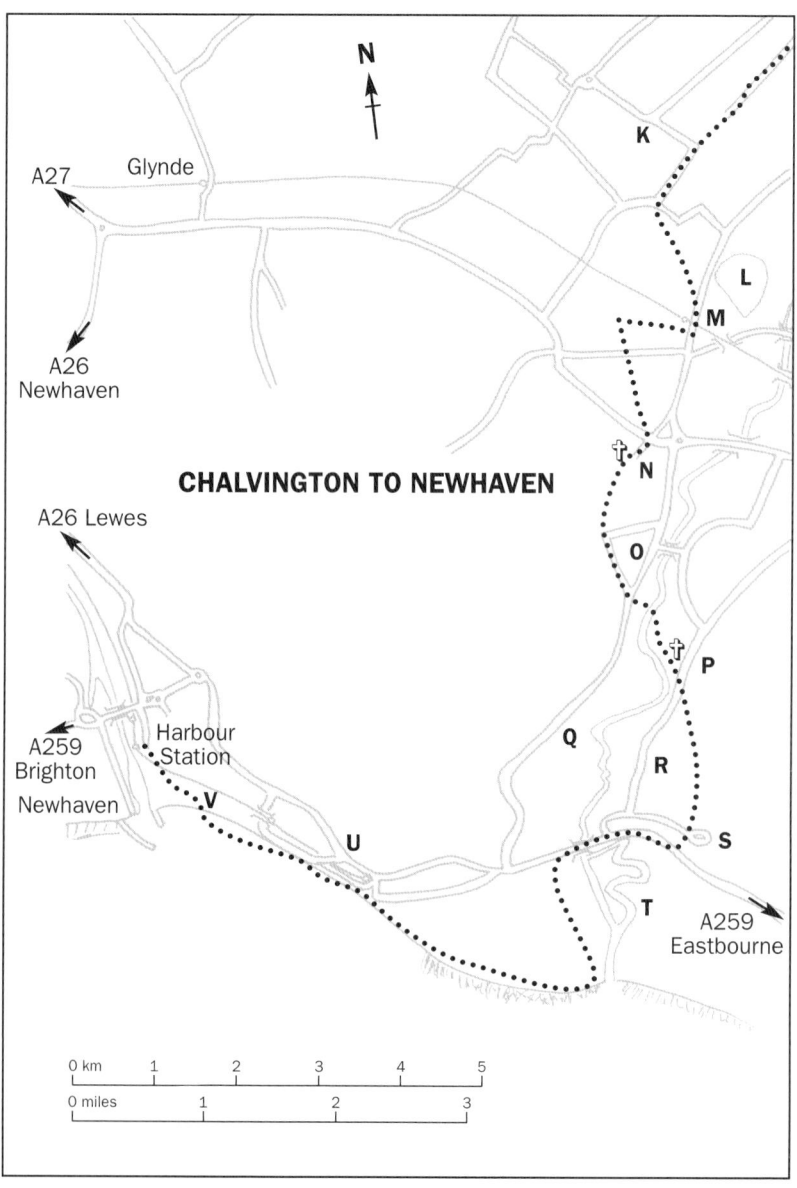

SECTION FIVE

ALFRISTON TO NEWHAVEN
(9³/₄ miles/15.6km)

And so, perhaps, to the most dramatic section! The Way follows the route of the South Downs Way as it leaves Alfriston along the banks of the river Cuckmere as far as Litlington, and then on past Charleston Manor and into the picturesque hamlet of Westdean. At Exceat the two Ways part company as our route makes for the photogenic fishermen's cottages at the mouth of Cuckmere Haven, and then follows the cliff tops over Seaford Head before dropping down to Splash Point at the eastern end of Seaford promenade. Past Tide Mills the Way follows the railway to Newhaven Harbour station and journey's end.

Leave Alfriston by turning off left down River Lane, opposite the market cross, crossing the river and proceeding along its bank as far as the next bridge. A right turn here back across the river will lead to the YHA hostel at Frog Firle, but the main route turns left into Litlington (**P**).

A pretty little village of Saxon origin, its name meaning quite simply *"Little Homestead"*. It has the distinction of having the county's original tea gardens, for it was here that Mr Russell introduced the first at the turn of the twentieth century. The church was started by the Normans but finished virtually two centuries later, its windows framed with chalk. The roof is built of ancient beams and the font dates back half a millennium.

Toilets and refreshments are available either at the Tea Gardens or the Plough and Harrow public house. Limited parking in the village.

Turn right at the road past the Plough and Harrow public house, then left at the metalled track by Thatch Cottage and right through a kissing gate, climbing up to continue along the edge of the next field from where there are views of the White Horse (**Q**) cut into the side of High and Over on the right.

This 90-foot long figure was carved in the chalk hillside sometime during the 19th century, probably as a youthful prank, by James Pagden, his brother and a cousin. Cross over two stiles before following the path along the borders of three fields, then descend to a stile and take a sharp turn left along a narrow path. Cross over the drive into the rear of Charleston Manor (**R**) of which only a glimpse is possible. Domesday Book recorded the manor of Norman origin, standing in beautiful gardens which are sometimes open to the public. A Tudor wing was added to the original house and a Georgian front was built between 1710-30.

Up some rough steps then along a forest path before turning right at the yellow waymarker, and passing the Glebe to Forge Cottage. The little village of Westdean (**S**) is off to the left, and it is possible to take the short detour round the village, rejoining the main route opposite the pond.

Alfred the Great is said to have owned a palace here but no traces of it have so far been discovered. The oldest inhabited house in Sussex - probably Britain - still exists, however, with parts dating back to 1220

Vanguard Way leaving Hope Gap with the Seven Sisters in the background.

with flint and stone walls almost 3 inches thick. Indeed most of the buildings in the village are built of flint.

The church of All Saints dates back to the Saxons although most of it is 14th century. Below the church is a pigeon tower and a massive flint wall - all that remains of the ancient manor house of the Thomas family who have a monument in the church. Cars are discouraged from entering the village, which is a tranquil place and a marvellous piece of unspoilt England.

Ascend the 215 steps of the long staircase, turning right at the wall from where there are magnificent views across Cuckmere Haven (**T**).

The Seven Sisters Country Park covers the lower part of the Cuckmere Valley and part of the Seven Sisters cliffs and is owned and managed by East Sussex County Council. There was once quite an important little fishing village nestling near the mouth of the River Cuckmere called Exceat but repeated incursions by French raiding parties following the ravages of the Black Death in 1348/9 caused the population to decline to virtual extinction by the early 16th century.

The Saxons were obviously here for the Cuckmere is named from a Saxon word meaning *"flowing water"* when it was much wider than today. Before that it was known as the River Exe from which the now lost village was named.

Over the stile in the wall and descend to a kissing gate behind the Visitor Centre to the A259 where there are bus stops for Eastbourne, Seaford and Brighton. Cross the road and continue right alongside it as far as the Golden Galleon Inn over the bridge, turning left through the car park and proceeding ahead towards the cottages on the skyline. Here you can witness one of the finest coastal views in Britain, the Seven Sisters headland. Follow the green path round the cliff top, past Hope Gap and the beacon atop Seaford Head, which looks something like a flying saucer but is in fact part of air traffic control's guidance system. Begin the steep descent to Splash Point, finally reaching the promenade by a gravel track. Keep ahead along the seafront at Seaford (**U**) past the Martello Tower to the point where the road swings off right.

Until the time of the Tudors Seaford was a thriving harbour at the mouth of the river Ouse, and a member of the Cinque Ports. Tradition then has it that in 1579 a terrible storm altered the course of the river causing it to enter the Channel at what we know today as Newhaven. But this is not the true story. What really happened was around 1539 the landowners of the Ouse valley were anxious to reclaim its marshes so they dug a new channel to divert the river so that it emerged instead at Meeching - and this they renamed 'Newhaven'. The terrible storm that wasn't was in fact an act of ruthless greed which condemned Seaford to what one historian called 'a state of living death'. The area between the esplanade and the town was once filled by wharves and quays, but the only medieval building to survive today is the church. Come the end of the Victorian era it suddenly became popular with retired people, eventually developing into the sedate little resort which it is today. Continue ahead past the sailing club, turning off right along a raised bank to Tide Mills (**V**).

There was a small community at Tide Mills as recently as the 1930s, although the cottages, whose walls and footings can be clearly seen, had no water, sanitation or power supply. The mills were begun in 1762 and, before they were closed in 1890, were able to use tidal energy for up to sixteen hours a day. What was once a bustling place is now a desolate, marshy site, but it is still possible to walk through the deserted streets to inspect the remnants of an industrial past.

Keep to the right of the lagoon, squeezed in by the railway as it comes in on the right. Cross the line by the footbridge, following the path to the station by Newhaven Harbour. This is journey's end, but follow the road for Newhaven town centre.

The Seven Sisters at the mouth of Cuckmere Haven.